Exposing the Pain

My Path to Freedom

Sharon M. Harris

AuthorHouse™
1663 Liberty Drive, Suite 200
Bloomington, IN 47403
www.authorhouse.com
Phone: 1-800-839-8640

© *2009 Sharon M. Harris. All rights reserved.*

No part of this book may be reproduced, stored in a retrieval system, or transmitted by any means without the written permission of the author.

First published by AuthorHouse 6/30/2009

ISBN: 978-1-4343-5256-9 (sc)

Printed in the United States of America
Bloomington, Indiana

This book is printed on acid-free paper.

Dedication

I thank my Lord and Savior Jesus Christ, who I love, worship and adore. He is my very present help whenever I need Him and constant companion whose daily fellowship is priceless. He is a friend who has been closer to me than my natural mother. He is my heavenly Father who replaced the pain of an absent earthly father with wholeness, completeness, and confidence. He is my teacher and instructor through the power of the Holy Spirit. Because of whom He has revealed Himself to be in my life, I am forever indebted to the man in the person of Jesus Christ. I'm completely sold out to do the Master's will. I have been privileged to be called His servant, yet chosen to be a joint heir of His riches and royalty. God handpicked and predestined me to inherit His kingdom; it was not because of my own righteous deeds, but His unmerited and divine favor bestowed upon me through His precious and priceless holy blood.

> *"But God, who is rich in mercy, because of His great love with which He loved us, even when we were dead in trespasses, made us alive together with Christ (by grace you have been saved), and raised us up together, and made us sit together in the heavenly places in Christ Jesus, that in the ages to come He might show the exceeding riches of His grace in His kindness toward us in Christ Jesus. For by grace you have been saved through faith, and that not of yourselves; it is the gift of God, not of works, lest anyone should boast…But now in Christ Jesus you who once were far off have been made near by the blood of Christ" (Ephesians 2:4-9, 13.)*

Oh how I love Jesus! It brings me great joy to be graced with the wonderful privilege to dedicate my book to my Master and King, Jesus Christ. Through Him, this book was published; and without Him, I could do nothing.

Extra Special Thanks

To my wonderful and loving husband, Mr. Harry Harris, Sr.: Your prayers and encouragement have been the strength I have needed to endure life's trials. I truly thank God for choosing me to be a part of His plan in your life. Words could never express the deep and unfathomable love I have for you. God has truly blessed me to be highly favored to have such a wonderful and great man of God like you.

Bishop Dwight McDaniels and Mother Marie McDaniels: The two of you may never know what an impartation you have deposited into my life; nevertheless, God knows. I love you both more than either of you could ever imagine. Thank you for allowing God to use you in such a way that has radically changed (and is still changing) my life as I continue to grow from glory to glory. The two of you have taught me how to endure hardship as a good soldier in the Lord and to never compromise holiness. Through solid biblical teaching, I have been able to hold up the bloodstained banner of righteousness and true holiness, regardless of the cost.

To my dearest and closest friend, Miss Donna Adams: I love you, girl. Thank you seems so inadequate for all the support and strength I have drawn from you. Thank you for loving me, and allowing me to just be me. You are truly an awesome woman of God!

Elder Edward Harris and Sister Sonya Harris: Your boldness to share Christ with me and your prayers brought your sister through some rough times. I truly thank God that He has so graciously ordained us not only to be related in the spiritual realm, but also in the natural. Thank you, big brother and sister.

To five of the most important people in my life, I do say, "Thank You." Dominic, Jamina, Jennifer, Jecoliah, and Harry Jr., I love you more than words can define. You have all been my reason to pursue my dreams and goals. I trust that I have demonstrated by example that you can achieve anything with God as the head of your lives.

Lovingly,
In Christ Service, Sharon

In Loving Memory

In loving memory of my father, Wilbur L. Hunter, who went home to be with the Lord in January of 1991. He came to know Jesus as His Lord and Savior before His death so he now awaits His loved ones in heaven. He lived the final portion of His days as a true and fervent Christian. His goal was to win one million souls to Jesus. The seeds of the Gospel message continue to produce even in my life. I believe the harvest will be great and His goals will be met.

Contents

Section 1 – Autobiography

CHAPTER 1
Where is my Momma and Daddy? 1

CHAPTER 2
Who am I? Why was I born? 9

CHAPTER 3
Death Trap of Rejection 15

CHAPTER 4
Touched by an Angel: A Miracle of Love 19

CHAPTER 5
Lost, But Not Forgotten 23

CHAPTER 6
The God of Mercy 27

CHAPTER 7
Salvation 33

Section 2 – Devotional: Three Women's Path To Freedom

CHAPTER 8
Girlfriend, What is your issue? 41

CHAPTER 9
The Living Water 45

CHAPTER 10
You Are Forgiven 49

Concluding Thoughts 53

Forward

I've had the privilege and honor to witness my sweetheart being changed by the manifest presence of God. Through the many years we have been married, her prayers and persistent study of God's word have totally transformed her from a fearful and insecure young lady into; a bold, confident, powerful, and passionate women for our Lord, Jesus Christ. You are truly a woman after God's own heart! Harry, your loving husband.

Optimistic, benevolent, and assurance to move mountains are just a few words that help me describe my mother. She has given me the key ingredients for the recipe to success. The main ingredients are One, accepting Jesus Christ as your Lord and Savior. Second, put God first in everything you do. Third, know that with God all things are possible. Last, live each day as if it was your last because tomorrow is not promised. She has demonstrated throughout her everyday life that God will give you the strength to do what's right according to His word if you want to be kept. She is an awesome mother, girlfriend, and woman of God to me. I feel comforted and protected in her presence. I love you mama, your oldest daughter Jamina

To the most beautiful woman in the world, the woman that God has sent to the earth to be an advocate for truth in these perilous times. Sharon Marie Harris is the most humble, compassionate, selfless, faithful, and giving woman I know. My mom has constantly reminded me of Gods love, and He is the only one who can permanently break the chains of sin. She believes that holiness and sanctification are important keys to establishing a healthy relationship with the Lord. She lives a life completely sold out for Jesus. The Lord's grace and mercy has raised her up out of the miry pit, and closed the mouths of the roaring lions. In the most adverse and uncertain times, she has stood firm on the rock of Jesus. I'm not boasting in Sharon Marie Harris, but I'm lifting of the name of Jesus Christ that lives inside this woman. I'm blessed to have her influence on my life as a friend, a sister and most of all, my mom. I love you mama and thank you for your love, encouragement, dedication, patience and most of all your desire to serve the Lord. Your oldest son, Dominic

There are simply three words that describe my mother, Sharon Harris: diligent, persistent, and a true woman of God. My mother has always believed in walking the walk, not talking the talk. She continues to exemplify this in her life as a Christian. She has demonstrated God's faithfulness even when I was not faithful to Him. Because of my mother, I know God's love is unfailing, never ending and unconditional. I am so grateful to God that my mother has truly been an example to me. No mothers' love have been greater than yours Mom! I love you so much and I'm so proud of you. Your second daughter, Jennifer

Beauty for Ashes is all I can think about when I read The Sharon Harris Story. Strength, faith, and hope are mere words that express only a fraction of what you have imparted into my life. I know that

God will use this book for His glory and allow many to come to the saving knowledge of Jesus Christ. How beautiful are the feet of them who preach the Gospel of peace. Romans 10:15 With Love from your youngest daughter, Jecoliah

My mother is a great person and she has set an example for me all of my life. I have seen people being set free from all types of bondages as a result of her willingness to obey God. She has helped so many women by telling them to "Expose the Pain", and receive God's healing anointing. I believe Sharon Harris is one of the greatest women of God in our lifetime. I really love you Mom, your youngest son, Harry Jr.

Introduction

In the summer of 1995 while preparing to speak at a youth banquet, the Spirit of the Lord spoke specifically to me saying, "Expose the Pain." Many of the Lord's people live behind a mask, failing to be freed from the bondages of a dysfunctional childhood. Shame and fear of rejection are the underlining factors in many cases. Christ will completely set you free from all of the pain endured as the result of traumatic events.

"Therefore if the Son makes you free, you shall be free indeed." (John 8:36)

No longer will you have to live your life plagued by haunted memories of a painful past; Jesus Christ will make your life worth living. Through an intimate relationship with Him, you will experience peace that passes all human understanding...

"...and the peace of God, which surpasses all understanding, will guard your hearts and minds through Christ Jesus" (Philippians 4:7)

...and joy unspeakable and full of glory.

"...whom having not seen you love. Though now you do not see Him, yet believing, you rejoice with joy inexpressible and full of glory." (1 Peter 1: 8)

As I expose my own personal pain, it will release faith, hope, and healing to you, the listener. You can also experience victory over every sin of your past that has caused you to live in shame, guilt and fear of rejection. You will find out that God has a purpose and a wonderful plan for your life that He is longing to reveal to you. I encourage you to read this book with great expectation and anticipation, knowing that your miracle for closure in many areas of your life will finally be resolved. Perhaps you have a loved one in desperate need of emotional healing; I encourage you to share this book with them in faith; trusting and believing God for their deliverance.

The story you are about to read is a real life portrayal of a young girl's disturbing formative years, which drove her to live a life beyond belief. All of the events in this book are true occurrences. Please allow Jesus to minister healing and hope to you regardless of your hopeless situation.

> ***"Now may the God of hope fill you with all joy and peace in believing, that ye may abound in hope, through the power of the Holy Ghost." (Romans 15:13)***

Get ready to receive the kind of peace that can only come from God. Just as He has delivered me, surely He will do the same for you, my dear friend!

> ***Jesus said, "Peace I leave with you, my peace I give unto you, not as the world giveth, give I unto you. Let not your heart be troubled neither let it be afraid." (John 14:27)***

Section 1 – Autobiography

CHAPTER 1

Where is my Momma and Daddy?

When my father and my mother forsake me, Then the LORD will take care of me. Psalms 27:10

Imagine if you would for a moment the image of a frightened little girl who was desperately in need of acceptance and affection. There I was, scared and all alone. My intense cries and desperate pleas fell upon deaf ears. It seemed that nobody could hear my internal and external cries for help. Or was it just that everyone around me that I needed really did not even care about me? I became frustrated as I searched for the true meaning of love. My diligent search began within my own family. "Surely," I thought to myself, "I must be able to find love in my own house. Why, I have three brothers and two sisters, so I'm never really alone." But in reality, although our house was always full of people, the wall of separation between our family members prohibited any meaningful communication. I was confused because I could not understand the anguish and pain in my little, lonely, broken heart. I kept trying to reach out to my momma, but my attempts went ignored. "Momma," I would cry, "please love me. I want to be accepted. I need you to hold me. I am only six years old, and I need my Momma."

I loved Momma so dearly that I would do anything to get her

attention and affection, whether it was positive or negative. The psychological thirst within me cried out for fulfillment, but Momma failed to attend to my emotional and spiritual needs. My mental perception and comprehension of love became greatly distorted. I would envision families being just like the ones they showed on the television. I watched as the Mommas on television held and caressed their little girls. "Why doesn't my Momma ever hug me?" I wondered, "Will she ever want to kiss my cute, fat little cheeks?"

I longed so deeply to just sit on my Momma's lap and lay my head on her chest. It was only a fantasy that never became a reality. Momma chose not to accept the physiological bond that should have came at the time of my birth. This act of rejection prohibited any future emotional attachments to develop between us.

Reminiscing, I wandered throughout our neighborhood becoming exposed to imagery that momma should have shielded me from. I would walk many blocks at any given time without any adult supervision. Once I became frightened, whether by nightfall or I had gone to far from home, I quickly turn around hoping I would remember the route in which I had traveled. I hurried home one particular day, a really tall man was holding a shining silver coin. He was standing in the doorway of a vacant house. Nevertheless, I was so fascinated with the coin because its power appeared to have a mesmerizing effect upon me. I was being lured into the vacant house by that coin the man was holding; fortunately, just before I came within arms reach of the really tall man, I snapped out of that hypnotic state. I quickly turned around and started running with all my might! I cried and cried, saying "I want my momma, I want my momma!"

Looking back with hindsight, my momma did the best she knew how to do with what she had. She only had a fourth grade education, no parenting skills, and by age 16 she had three children. Momma was on a path that was destined for doom. Her own physical, sexual, mental/emotional abuse caused severe damage to her wounded soul. I can only imagine that she had nowhere to turn and no support systems in place. Out of her wounded and bruised brain her priorities became twisted. Momma's priorities were first, drugs and alcohol; second, an assortment of disgusting and deplorable men; and last on her list of priorities always seemed to be her six children. Because it was evident that Momma loved drugs, alcohol, and partying more than she loved me, the black hole in my heart grew larger as I grew older.

The rejection from birth would be the pattern in which I would follow. Momma refused to accept me, or give me any positive affection. I don't remember one hug or kiss growing up as a child. I was the baby of our family and the black sheep of the family. I was treated accordingly and felt like the forgotten one who stuck out like a sore thumb. I felt like a misfit trying to find my way on a mixed up path in a mixed up family.

I could not give up. I made another attempt at finding what real love was. Reluctant, but determined, I tried reaching my arms and heart out to my Daddy. Although Daddy did not live with me, I was sure that at least he loved me. Daddy would occasionally visit me on the weekends, except for the times when Momma and Daddy would begin an argument of some sort. During those times, he would disappear and would not visit for three months or so. It actually felt like it was an eternity. I always seemed to experience such a deep sadness when I did not receive regular visits from Daddy. In spite of all the turmoil and confusion that occurred, I continued to try to convince myself that at least Daddy loved me. After all, of all my siblings, my sister and I were the only two that had the same biological father that would come to visit. The other three fathers never came to visit my sister or brothers. My siblings never received a present or even a birthday card from their daddies. Sad to admit, I felt special during those times of sibling rivalry, when I was able to attack them by saying, "at least I have a Daddy who loves and cares about me."

My siblings would shout at me, screaming horrible accusations about my Daddy. The alleged accusations that he physically and sexually abused them were more than I could bear. I would cover my ears and cry in disbelief. They were only saying this because they were jealous. Weren't they?

Tommy was my youngest brother. He accused my Daddy of placing his hands in the fire on the top of our gas stove, just because he wouldn't stop scratching. Tommy suffered from the skin disease called eczema… it was the worst case of eczema imaginable.

Sonny and Hedrick were my two eldest brothers. They claimed the constant physical abuse that came from the man I called Daddy almost drove them to kill him. My two brothers were literally destroying the image I had of a kind and loving Daddy.

Momma aided in the destruction process by constantly telling me a horrible story about the detailed acts of Daddy's alleged abuse. The accusations included incest, child abuse and domestic violence while the two were married. Momma claimed that my Daddy's erratic behavior was due to his alcoholism. I was only four years old when my parents divorced. The memory of Daddy living with the family was very vague. I do remember that Momma screamed and cried a lot. When Daddy finally moved out of our home, he never came back to live there again. I also remember watching Daddy as he consumed large quantities of alcohol. I witnessed my kind and loving Daddy turn into a person I did not know.

One night Daddy took me and my sister (Teddy Bear) from

my momma. Apparently, it was against her wishes because she was screaming at him and told him not to take us girls with him. He ignored her wishes and took us anyway. Daddy said we were going to San Diego where he lived and we would live with him for a while. Before we arrived at his house, Daddy made a stop at a local bar and told me and my sister that he would be right back. Daddy didn't come right back but many hours passed by as I lay on the back seat of Daddy's black and white 4dr car. I remember flashing lights and stumbling men and women coming out of the front door of the bar. Finally, daddy came out of the bar stumbling like the other people and began to drive us to his house. I remember Daddy almost hitting other cars and side swiping a parked car. I witnessed my kind and loving Daddy turn into a person I did not know.

On another occasion, I met a really nice friend. I was only five years old because I didn't attend school all day. It was half a day kindergarten. My first friend was such a nice lady and I really trusted her. She was my daily crossing guard and made sure I would make it safe across the busy boulevard. Even though I would chance running across the busy boulevard when she wasn't there, I always felt protected when she held my hand and escorted me across the street. One day the crossing guard, my first friend, asked me to rub her forehead. She said that she suffered from severe migraine headaches. I quickly agreed to help my friend because I didn't want her to suffer from the pain she described. So, after I would cross the street, the crossing guard would open the passenger door of her car instructing me to get in, and shut the door. After she would get in on the drivers side, I would scoot as close as possible to her and began rubbing her forehead. My first friend was a very light completed lady and when she would have these headaches she would be beak red, with watery eyes. I would rub, rub, and rub; until she dozed off. She would always reward me with a piece of fruit, candy or a whole quarter. She would say to me that you always stop the pain for me, you having healing in your hands. Even though I didn't understand what she was talking about, this went on for a long time; and then she just disappeared and I never saw her again. She made me feel like a person with a purpose in life, and I felt very special. The thought of having the potential to heal a person made me feel like I had some special power that God gave to me and maybe I was born to be one of God's earthly helpers.

This was also the years of the big rats that ran around our house. The rats were so big that they resembled newborn kittens. I remember hearing my brother scream one night because a rat had crawled in bed with him. Whether he was bitten or not I don't remember, all I know is that I was absolutely terrified of those nasty fat crawling and creepy creatures! Sleeping on the bottom bunk was a nightmare all by itself. I wet the bed because I was too afraid to go to the bathroom to use it because in my five year old mind I thought I would be eaten alive by a rat. Well, I will never forget my live encounter with the Papa rat. It was still day light outside, and I was heading for my bedroom when all of a sudden I saw this huge rat running past me. I ran and hopped on top of the dining room table and screamed as loud as my lungs would allow me. I was crying and trembling in sheer terror. Mr. Avery, one of Momma's boyfriends came running out of the back bedroom. The rat was trying to eat the cheese off the rat trap in the corner, when Mr. Avery hit the rat, scaring it off. I knew at that moment my life was saved, but I hated those big fat rats. I thought is normal for rats to invade our home; however, that house was eventually condemned and became an empty lot; 8830 Orchard Ave. was the first address I remembered. I thought I was a big girl because I knew the name of my street and the number. The only other street name prior to that address I could remember was Estrella. Ms. Mable was my god-mother, who always smelled like rubbing alcohol, and she was the one responsible for my crazy nickname I absolutely hated; Fakey May Jones! What a ridiculous name when I was called by that name. My god-mother use to talk like a baby and stumble every time I would see her.

It was summer time fun in 1970, splashing in the pool, screaming, running, and jumping in the sparkling cool water at Manchester Park. I was a kid on a mission and fun was all I could think about all day and everyday during those times in the hot California summer days. My brother, Tommy was a junior life guard and dared me to jump into the pool on the deep end. Fearfully, I reminded him that I didn't know how to swim. He reassured that I would be safe because he was a junior life guard and very much aware that I didn't know how to swim. As my heart was racing because of fear, I foolishly jumped in the 8 feet deep water and I was only about 4 feet tall. I began drowning hoping that my brother would fulfill his promise to save me. He thought the appearance of my drowning was the funniest site and was too engaged in his laughing fit to rescue me. I was fighting for my life! I drank so much chlorine filled water and fighting so hard for my young life. My oldest sister (Mimi) started screaming! "Somebody save her!" and then jumped into the pool attempting to save me but she just couldn't get me under control to rescue me. Amidst all of the commotion, a senior life guard dove in the pool and rescued me. All I remember is literally hearing a trumpet, my belly being pumped, choking, and throwing up water. Fortunately, I became fully conscious before I actually died and I was not permitted back in the pool that particular day. The time of fun ended in tragedy which would unfortunately be a patterned in which I would live my life.

CHAPTER 2

Who am I? Why was I born?

For I know the thoughts and plans that I have for you, says the Lord, thoughts and plans for welfare and peace and not for evil, to give you hope in your final outcome. Then you will call upon Me, and you will come and pray to Me, and I will hear and heed you. Then you will seek Me, inquire for, and require Me [as a vital necessity] and find Me when you search for Me with all your heart. Jeremiah 29:11-13

Oh, how I wished I could make things right. I longed for the remedy that would heal my dysfunctional home. I struggled to find my true identity. Because my life was empty, I lived without a purpose. The environment I lived in caused me to adopt role models that were alcoholics and drug addicts. There were countless nights I would lay awake listening to the loud commotion from a wild party. I reasoned within myself that the people present were experiencing overwhelming joy; despite the fact that the parties would always end very violently. Feeling helpless and frightened, I would try to escape those sad and pathetic events by cuddling up at night next to my sister Sonya, who was like my own real live Teddy Bear. Those were the moments in my life when I felt safe. It seemed as though everything would be all right while I was hiding under the covers with her by my side, but morning would always come and the reality of my life was inescapable. It was all too real.

Hopelessness and despair filled my heart.

There were many sleepless nights because of the constant chaos going on in my home. I hated the very essence of the degrading behavior I was surrounded by, but it appeared to be the norm. Trapped in the midst of confusion, I was being suctioned into a cycle of learned sinful behavior, unfairly taught to my defenseless little mind. This opened up doors to demonic strongholds in my life that could only be broken by the power of God.

I watched in horror as my brother (Sonny) foamed from his mouth threatening to kill himself and others around him. I didn't understand what was happening to my oldest brother. However, while several people were holding him down on the floor in our living room and amongst all the commotion, I over-heard someone say that my brother was having a bad trip on the Angel Dust. This was the same drug that my mother's brother was on when he jumped through several apartment windows while he was under the influence of Angel Dust which in known as PCP also. My uncle barely escaped death and when I saw him, he had cuts, stitches, and was bandaged from head to toe. I couldn't understand why anyone would give that drug to my brother. Because of the constant horror stories about family, friends, and neighbors who went crazy while under the influence of drugs, there was a desensitizing effect it had on my very immature mind. I wondered if I was born and destined to experience the same fate as my older role models. Was that way I was born?

School days were extremely hard for me, and I dreaded having to get up early in the morning. In spite of all the confusion going on in my life I managed to excel academically, but Momma ignored all of my academic achievements; therefore, my enthusiasm and motivation diminished. In desperation, I began reaching out to my grade school teacher by writing her letters. I expressed my need for love and affection, but once again my attempts failed. I soon realized that my teacher seemed only interested in the very pretty girls. Mrs. Trinity would host special events at her home and only invited her pretty little princesses. During auditions for school plays, I would tell my teacher that I wanted to participate, but her reply would be "you are too fat and dark-complexioned." The remarks of Mrs. Trinity aided in the destruction process. I had no self-esteem, and I was left feeling lonely, hopeless, and in despair. By the time I was in the fifth grade, I began acting upon all of the frustration and anger going on inside of me. I was very bitter and began getting into a tremendous amount of trouble at school. I would get into fight after fight, making a bad reputation for myself; nevertheless, the attention felt pretty good. This was the first time in my life that I was finally gaining notoriety. I learned quickly how to manipulate any given situation to get my way and used that as a tool. My self-defined philosophy was that if I wanted something, I would not ask for it, I would just take it.

By the end of my fifth grade school year, life at home was very bad. Momma was barely at home. During the few times she was there, she had different men spending nights at our house. Many of her boyfriends were disgraceful drunks. One of my mother's boyfriends would drink until he would vomit uncontrollably and pass out. I was sexually assaulted by a few of Momma's boyfriends. One night Momma was having a party and a strange man came into my bedroom. As he began to sexually assault me, Momma entered the room. She was very intoxicated and casually told this boyfriend of hers to come back to the party in the other room. I tried to tell Momma what was happening, but she told me to shut up and go to sleep. Those were the times I felt all bottled up with mixed emotions. I loved Momma, but I also hated her. I began to harbor a great deal of anger, bitterness and resentment towards Momma. I could not figure out why Momma was not there for me.

The security and protection that came from a mother's love was foreign to me. When I was 9 years old, I told Momma that I was in lots of pain due to constipation. Her boyfriend suggested that I drink some cheap wine and it would work just like a laxative. The ridiculous prescription could have killed me. I consumed so much alcohol under the instruction of Momma's boyfriend that I passed out. After vomiting and then having a severe headache that followed, I slept for two days straight.

Because of the lack of discipline, I was at liberty to do whatever I wanted. Eventually, I began to associate with the wrong crowd. I felt special because I found acceptance with all of my rejected friends. By age 11, our family was about to completely crumble. Momma had decided she wanted to live her life apart from her six children. She claimed that she was tired of being a single parent. Momma said, "I never enjoyed my childhood because I started having you children at a very young age."

Momma was tired of struggling with six children on her own. There were many broken relationships with men, rebellious adolescences, and enormous financial problems which led to poverty. Yes, momma was the womb in which carried me throughout the 9 months of pregnancy, but God was my creator who conceived me with a purpose before I ever entered the earth. His loving hand would lead me to Him, and His divine interventions had already designed my destiny. Out of the ruins of death, my heavenly daddy would deliver me.

My questions in life remained unanswered until His love sought me out and found me. Only God knows the beginning to the end, for God's love reached throughout eternity into time manifesting His love in the person of Jesus Christ, the redeemer, giver of life, and revealer of purpose.

Why was I born? Who am I? A reflection of God's most lovely and prized possession created in His very image and a manifestation of His wonderful handiwork. Only time would allow this powerful truth to be revealed to me and totally transform my future forever.

> *And the LORD God formed man of the dust of the ground, and breathed into his nostrils the breath of life; and man became a living soul. Gen. 2:7*

> *LORD, you have searched me [thoroughly] and have known me. You know my downsitting and my uprising; You understand my thought afar off. You sift and search out my path and my lying down, and You are acquainted with all my ways. For there is not a word in my tongue [still unuttered], but, behold, O Lord, You know it altogether. You have beset me and shut me in--behind and before, and You have laid Your hand upon me .Your [infinite] knowledge is too wonderful for me; it is high above me, I cannot reach it. Where could I go from Your Spirit? Or where could I flee from Your presence? If I ascend up into heaven, You are there; if I make my bed in Sheol (the place of the dead), behold, You are there. If I take the wings of the morning or dwell in the uttermost parts of the sea, Even there shall Your hand lead me, and Your right hand shall hold me. If I say, Surely the darkness shall cover me and the night shall be [the only] light about me, Even the darkness hides nothing from You, but the night shines as the day; the darkness and the light are both alike to You .For You did form my inward parts; You did knit me together in my mother's womb. I will confess and praise You for You are fearful and wonderful and for the awful wonder of my birth! Wonderful are Your works, and that my inner self knows right well .My frame was not hidden from You when I was being formed in secret [and] intricately and curiously wrought [as if embroidered with various colors] in the depths of the earth [a region of darkness and mystery]. Your eyes saw my unformed substance, and in Your book all the days [of my life] were written*

before ever they took shape, when as yet there was none of them. How precious and weighty also are Your thoughts to me, O God! How vast is the sum of them! If I could count them, they would be more in number than the sand. When I awoke, [could I count to the end] I would still be with You. Psalm 139:1-18

CHAPTER 3
Death Trap of Rejection

Before I formed you in the womb I knew [and] approved of you [as My chosen instrument], and before you were born I separated and set you apart, consecrating you; [and] I appointed you as a prophet to the nations. Jeremiah 1:5

I was not alone; my siblings also experienced the harsh reality of abandonment and rejection. My oldest sister Deborah was killed because of Momma's neglect. Momma had stayed out all night partying and before dozing off to sleep, she had placed a large pot of water on the stove. The water was boiling and my three eldest siblings ran around the kitchen table. The large pot fell off the stove and landed on Momma's first-born child. The burns that Deborah received were so severe that she only lived three days after the accident. My precious oldest sister was only four years old when this tragic event happened. Unfortunately, this was one of many tragic events Momma had to endure without any mental or emotional support. Momma talked little about Deborah and it was only when she appeared intoxicated that she would tearfully reminisce about her pain of losing her first born. It was apparent that Momma was broken, battered and bruised; however she used drugs and alcohol to erase her pain. Although I was not yet born, the vicious cycle of child endangerment and neglect would continue.

My oldest brother Sonny struggled all of his life with drug addiction. His drug addiction started when he was very young. His involvement with gangs and crime often caused him to remain in trouble with the law. Sonny was fifteen when he used a street drug named PCP, and he completely lost control. He threatened to kill himself and everyone around him. His addiction escalated, and by age twenty, he was shooting drugs intravenously. Sonny was desperately trying to escape all of the pain he was experiencing due to our dysfunctional upbringing. His addiction continued until his death in October of 1997. Sonny was only thirty-nine years old when he died.

My second oldest brother followed in Sonny's path using drugs. Hedrick was addicted to smoking marijuana by age twelve. To escape the horrors and hurt caused by our upbringing, Hedrick joined the United States Army. My brother was stationed in Germany. I received a few calls and one visit and then he disappeared, never to be seen or heard of again. It has been over twenty-five years since my brother disappeared.

Tommy, my youngest brother, was addicted to various types of prescription drugs and illegal street drugs. Eczema had taken over His whole body to the point he was unrecognizable. I was the only one who would take the time to rub medicine on His wounds as we were growing up. He would itch so terribly, that he would actually scratch the flesh off in certain areas. Momma told me it was because she had slept with a man, and it turned out that his wife was into witchcraft, so she cast a spell on Tommy. He also suffered from mental illness and was diagnosed as having manic depression. He lived most of his life in different unfit foster homes. Even there, he experienced a great deal of physical and mental abuse. He continued as a drug abuser until his death. He died at the young age of thirty from AIDS.

My oldest sister, Mimi, was a runaway and spent most of her childhood in various foster homes and the California Juvenile Detention Center. Momma had relinquished all parental rights concerning Mimi before she turned twelve years old. During the brief period my oldest sister was at home, I was very happy. I loved my sister dearly. We shared a special bond and I longed for us to stay together but it never happened. I wished that I could erase the enormous pain we both experienced during those terrible childhood years. My other sister, Teddy Bear (Sonya) went in a completely different direction, to church.

I was the youngest in our family and I lived my life in a callous manner, like a rebel without a cause. Many of my associates were involved in illegal drug use and distribution. I was living in the fast lane heading towards death and destruction. Growing up in South Central, Los Angeles made the situation worse. Murders, stabbings, and drive-by shootings were common occurrences. Many of my close acquaintances were brutally murdered due to senseless acts of violence. I felt as though all the odds were stacked against me and there was no way out of the death trap that surrounded me. Yet I found acceptance among this particular group of people. There was a common bond that we shared, and we could identify with each other's pain. We all felt like hopeless rejects.

Because I was living my life on the edge, by age twelve, I was pregnant and had nowhere to turn. I was abandoned, frightened and left all alone. It was not until the sixth month of my pregnancy that I realized something was extremely different about my body. I was so young and naïve that the last thing I suspected was being pregnant. I would experience something moving in my stomach, but it never occurred to me that it was a baby living inside of me. I was ten years old when my menstrual cycle started, and my friend told me that once your period starts, you could never become pregnant. I believed this information and ruled the possibility of pregnancy completely out.

I was too young to understand about the reproductive processes in life; even though I was actively involved in the process.

After my pregnancy was confirmed, the saga of pain and rejection continued, only this time I was the source. I directly caused pain, hurt, and shame to come upon my Daddy and myself. Lashing out in anger and bitterness, I sadly accused my Daddy of fathering my child. I thought within myself, "How could I be so cruel and callous to tell such a horrible and hideous lie?" Deep inside, all I wanted was Momma to love me. I felt like a contagious disease and such a horrible person. I would look in the mirror and tell myself how bad and disgraceful I was. Four weeks after my pregnancy was confirmed, my son Dominic was born.

CHAPTER 4

Touched by an Angel: A Miracle of Love

Be not forgetful to entertain strangers, for thereby some have entertained angels unawares. Hebrews 13:2

Everything that was happening in my life seemed like a dream that I would one day awaken from, but the events were a harsh reality. The doctor had to perform an emergency C-Section to deliver my son because I was so young and too small to deliver him. I was rushed to the hospital. While traveling in the car, I was bleeding uncontrollably. I slipped in and out of consciousness due to the loss of blood. Upon arriving at the hospital, I was raced down a hall and placed in a little room as the doctor prepared to do emergency surgery to save the lives of both my son and myself. The doctors told my mother that my son's chances of survival were slim to none, but he would do his very best to save my life. As I lay in this little room unconscious, I had a visit from a total stranger who touched my stomach and spoke gentle words that I couldn't understand.

When I woke up, I had given birth to a premature four-pound, ten-ounce baby boy. He was so tiny and fragile. He suffered from various health complications and had to be fed by a tube. Many of his major organs were under-developed because of improper prenatal nutrition. The first time the nurse brought my own, real live baby doll out to me, I was terrified. Nevertheless, the first time I held my son, I immediately bonded with him. I had not a clue about how to be a mother, but I was very aware that I loved that little boy more than words could express.

Everyone around me tried to convince me to give my son up for adoption. My family members, friends, and the nurse who cared for me while I stayed in the hospital were among the voices. The voices all around me were telling me that my son would have a better chance at life if I gave him up for adoption. I finally had a reason to live, and I was devastated at the thought of losing my son. The hospital refused to release my son into my custody and was going to place him in a foster home if one of my parents didn't sign legal documents. I begged my mother to please sign the forms so the state would not take my baby boy away, and she agreed. This was the first time I was really able to appreciate having a mother. As the months passed, by the time I was thirteen years old, my son and I were in separate foster homes. I became extremely depressed and failed at a suicide attempt. I didn't want to live without the only love of my life. This was a very difficult period in my life, and the only thing that sustained me was a scripture that I had learned in Vacation Bible School. The life changing verse was

> ***John 3:16, "For God so loved the world that he gave His only begotten son and whosoever believeth in him should not perish but have everlasting life."***

I was about seven years old when I attended the bible school for the first time. The bait that lured me was the cookies and punch, but the life-changing message of hope would later be the only source of strength I had. The teacher told me that God sent His son Jesus to die for me because he loves me so very much. Although I did not comprehend the reality of that powerful truth, the seed of the word of God was sown into my heart.

In spite of the shame and reproach I had brought on my father, accusing him of fathering my son, he forgave me and longed to be in my life, and the life of my son. My father loved Dominic. He could no longer watch His grandson remain separated from him. He asked for custody of my son, and I agreed. My father became my son's guardian and closest buddy until his death.

CHAPTER 5

Lost, But Not Forgotten

But God shows and clearly proves His [own] love for us by the fact that while Therefore, since we are now justified (acquitted, made righteous, and brought into right relationship with God) by Christ's blood, how much more [certain is it that] we shall be saved by Him from the indignation and wrath of God. Romans 5:8-9

I continued to live a life of promiscuity, and many of my associates were two-and-a-half times my age. I was only fourteen years old, and I was forced to become an adult. I was frightened and scared to death, with nowhere to turn. Barbie dolls, jump ropes, and hopscotch were just a flash of a memory. I found myself living the lifestyle that I despised watching as a child. I was trapped in a cycle of bondage and chains that was passed down in my family, from generation to generation. The curse of drug addiction lured me into its grip, because the use of drugs seemed to ease the pain. I was pregnant with my second child, a beautiful daughter. The man who fathered my daughter was extremely verbally and physically abusive. The beatings and mental torment became unbearable. After being rushed to an emergency room to receive stitches to repair a near- fatal head injury, I knew that I had to get out that relationship if I wanted to live.

Once again I was abandoned, and the feelings of hopelessness and despair filled my heart. I continued to think that my life would never amount to anything. I laid in the hospital bed as tears flowed down my cheeks. I started to believe that nothing good would become of my life, but the merciful hand of God was at work behind the scenes, setting my destiny in order. The Lord predestined my future in spite of the present mess my life was in. My sister Teddy Bear had become a Christian, and she had been praying long and hard for my deliverance. She continued to pray that God would send laborers in my path to share the plan of salvation with me.

By the time I was sixteen years old, I had lived such a fast paced lifestyle that it became evident that my life was nearing an end if I didn't change. I was heading for destruction and I became desperate for a way out of the grips of sin and shame. But I couldn't find the way out, so I had to keep drowning out the voices in my head.

One night, as I was getting high with my oldest sister, all of a sudden my heart started beating very fast and intense pain followed. I had already been awake for a couple of days partying and I was exhausted. I sat on the bed and began to scream, because I knew that I was about to die. I was terrified! My sister came into the room to find out what was wrong with me. I barely got the words out that I was about to die. She just said, "Girl, you'll be all right. Just get a little rest, and stop screaming! I'm trying to get high and you are messing my high up." When she left the room, I sat on the bed trying to pull myself together, and a tremendous heaviness came over me. This force had incredible strength and it seemed to overpower me. I slipped backwards and began falling into a hideous dark tunnel. The darkness was like no other darkness I had ever experienced. As I was falling backwards, the faces of my immediate family members began to flash before my very eyes. I screamed out in desperation, but it was to no avail. As I continued to fall, I saw a figure that looked like a man. This man was very far away, and he stood in an incredible light. He reached out His arms towards me and I immediately responded. I was about to touch His hands when I woke up. I jumped out of the bed and ran around the house, hoping that I was still alive. I later found out that I had overdosed from the use of cocaine. I was scared 'straight' from that horrifying situation, never to use cocaine ever again.

CHAPTER 6

The God of Mercy

Through the LORD's mercies we are not consumed, because His compassions fail not. They are new every morning; great is Your faithfulness. Lamentations 3:22 & 23

I continued to wander around the mean streets of South Central, Los Angeles looking for someone to love me. I was definitely looking for love in all the wrong places. I met a drug dealer who lavished me with elaborate gifts, and I was very impressed by his generosity. Chuck won my heart with his affection and his kindness. No person had ever treated me so special, so I was convinced that this relationship was true love. I later learned that Chuck was a liar, a cheater, and a dominating manipulator. Although I knew the truth, I convinced myself it was a lie. Deep within me, I knew this relationship was all wrong. He became very controlling, verbally and physically abusive and convinced me that no other man would ever love me and accept me. Sadly, I accepted his lies. After all, I had never been in any loving relationship before, and had no idea what love really meant.

Six months after my relationship began with Chuck, a psychotic man that had once lived in my neighborhood abducted me at gunpoint. The man had just been released from prison for second-degree murder. The man and his accomplice forced me into a car.

As I sat between the two men, a police car pulled up beside the car we were in. The psychotic man stated that if I screamed, he would kill me instantly. He taunted me with the echoing statement "I finally got you. You are going to see a real good movie, and you will be the star of the show." I knew within myself that my death was inevitable. Such despair flooded my heart and mind due to this inescapable knowledge. I arrived at the house where the movie was to take place, and I was terrified. I begged and pleaded for my life. The psychotic man laughed hideously. I begged the man to at least let me see my children for the last time, but he denied my request.

Not knowing what to do or where to turn, suddenly I remembered what I learned at Vacation Bible School. As I remembered back to when I was a little child, I could hear the very words of my teacher. She said that God truly loved me and sent His only son to die for me. Hope began to fill my heart because I started to believe that God would not let this man hurt me. I began to talk to God and I asked Him to please help me get out of this horrible situation and not die tormented. I asked the man again if he would please allow me to see my children, but once again he refused. I looked my abductor in the eyes and said, "Do you believe in God?" With a deep and terrifying voice, he responded, "I hate God! There is no God, and I don't care if I died tonight!" I was extremely petrified after hearing those words come out of this man's mouth. Only a fool would say such ridiculous words.

I asked the man once again to please allow me to see my children or at least call them. The man agreed to let me call my children. But instead of calling my children, I called Chuck, the drug dealer (my "boyfriend.") I was able to mutter under my breath, "He is going to kill me with his gun," and then I said louder, "How are the children doing?" Chuck said, "Where are you?" Suddenly, my abductor snatched the phone. I prayed to God, "Please spare my life and let me see my children again." All of a sudden, the man changed his mind and agreed to take me to see my children. He stated that it would be the last time I would ever see them. The ride to my home seemed to be the longest ride in my life, and so many thoughts flooded my mind. As soon as I entered my house, I picked up my baby girl, hugged her very tightly and began weeping. I asked my babysitter where my son was, and she stated that my father had decided to keep him another night.

It was nothing less than the merciful hand of God that my son was not in the house. A stray bullet would have probably hit him, taking into account all of the chaos that took place that night. My babysitter knew that something was terribly wrong. My abductor kept his hand inside his jacket, obviously holding his gun. He became very agitated and said, "Okay, that's enough time; let's go." I sadly put my daughter down. Suddenly there was a hard knock on the front door. I opened the door, and without any warning, gunfire erupted. I was in the midst of a shoot-out, and I actually felt the bullets graze my face. I grabbed my daughter to attempt to run into a little room nearby. I was close enough to be within arms reach of my abductor, who tried to shoot me while I ran with my daughter. I could not understand how he could miss me at such a close range.

I finally made it to the little room. I stood huddled in a corner, using my body as a human shield to protect my daughter. I could hear someone running throughout my house, throwing open every closet door. I did not know that it was my abductor. He was still alive in my house, looking for me, but he was severely wounded. Two shots came through the open door of the little room we were in, and I was terrified. My heart was beating so hard and fast that

I could literally hear the thumps. I closed my eyes as I heard the footsteps of my abductor entering the room. Suddenly, I heard a loud thump and I felt something on my feet. My abductor had dropped dead at my feet! He did not live long enough to carry out his plans to kill me. But God is rich in mercy, for His great love, wherewith He loved me and spared my life and the life of my daughter. My abductor died with his eyes wide open, and I remembered how he foolishly cursed God and stated that he didn't care if he died that very night. I was taken to the police station for questioning and I told them that I had killed my abductor. The police ruled the homicide as self-defense and dismissed all charges.

The truth was as follows: the knock on the door was Chuck. I opened the door and my abductor immediately started shooting. Chuck returned fire, striking him in the chest. Three months after this horrible ordeal, I was still trying to forget about it, but Chuck would not let me or my surroundings. Approximately two weeks after the shooting, I had to return home where the homicide took place. Having to clean all the blood was a living nightmare. There was blood splattered throughout that tiny little house, and it was a horrible bloody mess. On the kitchen floor where some blood had dried up, it had began to curl and I remembered sweeping large pieces into a dust pan. I was holding my breath because the stench was awful. Reflecting on that tragedy, I remembered feeling numb as I cleaned the blood that day. I knew I had to get over it because I had to live in the very house where the crime took place. Even though I desperately tried to bury that dreadful day, I was severely traumatized and tormented day and night. *"I was sleeping in the same room where the man died, I was walking in the same steps where I had to clean his blood, and every time I went to sleep I woke up terrified and screaming because I was constantly having flashbacks of that horrific event."* He constantly reminded me that he saved my life and that I should feel indebted to him. I told him that he was not the one who saved my life, but it was the God I heard about in Vacation Bible School. Nevertheless, the domination and control were blinding me from the truth. After several months of mental/emotional torture and being scared out of my wits, I agreed to move in with Chuck and the mother of His children. Shortly afterwards, I realized that this would be one of the worst mistake I've made in my life. They began to control every part of my life. I wasn't allowed to have any friends besides them. Our daily routine was to drink, do drugs, and listen to the blues. I was emotionally, spiritually and physically exhausted from the lifestyle I was living to the point that it was unbearable.

I had only been on this earth for sixteen short years and the trauma was driving me insane. I was suffocating in my own fluid, and I felt as though my head was barely above water. My lips were covered and my nose was burning; drowning in a deep sea, desperate, dark, cold and lonely. I was scared to death as my personal ship was sinking. It was half way down and I was holding on for dear life. I was screaming for someone to rescue my lost, battered, bruised and abused soul.

CHAPTER 7

Salvation

In this the love of God was made manifest (displayed) where we are concerned: in that God sent His Son, the only begotten or unique [Son], into the world so that we might live through Him. In this is love: not that we loved God, but that He loved us and sent His Son to be the propitiation (the atoning sacrifice) for our sins. 1John 4:9&10

One night while I was partying, I received a telephone call from my sister, Teddy Bear. She was about to marry a preacher that was very passionate and bold for God. She put him on the phone to talk to me, and he began to boldly proclaim that Jesus Christ is Lord, and he told me that Jesus could be my Lord, too. I immediately became sober and started to weep. He said...

"if I would confess with my mouth and believe in my heart that God raised Jesus Christ from the dead I would be saved. For with the heart man believeth unto righteousness and with the mouth confession is made unto salvation and whosoever call upon the name of the Lord shall be saved." (Romans 10:9, 10 &13)

He also said, "Sharon, Jesus will change your life. But until you totally surrender everything to him and come to the foot of the cross, your situation will never change." He confidently spoke words of faith, healing and hope to my lost and dying soul. He said, "Sharon, I am looking forward to seeing you real soon." As

I held onto the telephone, there was a silence in the room. My companions in the party stared at me, and the music stopped. The silence was broken when a female said, "You look like you have just seen a ghost."

Not many days after this experience, I was on a street corner waiting for the bus. A young preacher stood on the corner proclaiming the Gospel to the multitude of people who passed him daily. I was in a crowd that particular day and the man fixed his eyes on me and said, "Hey, young lady! The hand of God is upon your life, for he has a great calling upon you." He said some of the same words that my future brother-in-law had spoken not many days ago. I desperately wanted to change my life, so I asked the preacher to pray for me. He prayed that I would totally surrender my will to the will of God. I stood on that corner and wept bitterly. I just couldn't see any way out of my hopeless condition. He assured me that God is faithful and He would complete the work that He has already begun.

Not many days after that experience, I was in a terrible car accident and suffered a head concussion. As I lay on the ground, a man appeared and knelt down beside me. He told me that I was going to be all right and the ambulance was on the way. I was frightened, scared, and confused; but his gentle and soft-spoken words seemed to erase my anxiety. My girlfriend was the driver of the car. As she walked to the place where I was laying, she interrupted the man that was talking to me. She said, "Hey girl, play it off and we will get a lot of money." The man turned towards my girlfriend and said, "How dare you say such a thing? She could have been lost in eternity forever." My girlfriend was a very light-skinned young woman, but when she looked into the man's face, she turned very red and fearfully walked away. The man turned towards me and looked in my eyes as he held my hand and said, "Can't you see Jesus loves you so much. Please give your life to Jesus before it is too late." Arriving at the hospital, I wept bitterly as I lay in the bed alone. The words spoken by the total stranger echoed in my ears. There was no more doubt in my mind that God really loved me and wanted to save my sinful soul from hell. I tearfully and prayerfully asked Jesus Christ to come into my heart. I told God that I was ashamed for living such a sinful life. I had finally come to the place of total surrender. As I asked Jesus to wash and cleanse me with His precious blood, something miraculous happened. I instantly felt an enormous burden of heaviness lift off of my life. My life was completely transformed that very night. I would never return to the life I was living that was full of sin, guilt and shame.

Miraculously, I was not severely injured as a result of the car accident. Just as the total stranger had promised, I was okay. I was released from the hospital the next day. I was determined to allow God to change the way I was living.

Upon arriving at the house where I was living, I announced to Chuck and the mother of his children I was a new Christian and I was moving out tonight. Chuck immediately locked the barred security door, which had a dead bolt and headed for his bedroom in the back of the house. The mother of his children rushed to the kitchen and grabbed a butcher knife from the drawer. I stood in the living room holding my daughter's hand; I was in utter disbelief that the people I deemed as family would do such horrible things to me. She put the butcher knife to my throat, and threatened to kill me if I left. She stated, "You promised that you would never leave us." Chuck was returning from the back of the house, and in his right hand, he was holding the same .357 magnum gun that had killed my abductor. I was speechless and terrified because I did not know if I would leave the house alive. I began to pray silently. An overwhelming peace came upon me, and I knew God was with me; therefore, I would be safe. She slowly removed the knife from my throat, and without any warning, she punched me in my left eye. Chuck immediately grabbed her arm and said, "Let her go, she will be back." He walked over to the door and unlocked it. I swiftly exited the house with my daughter. After walking out of that house, the harsh reality was I had nowhere to go. Hopelessness and dread flooded my soul and I began to weep. I rode the public bus for several hours and finally decided to go to my mother's house. No one answered so I sat on the steps. As I cuddled up with my daughter, a door opened behind me. A young woman said that the Lord woke her up and said, "There is a young girl with her baby outside, you must bring her into your home." The young woman gave my daughter a bath and fed us some rice with butter, topped with sugar. After she made sure our physical needs were met, she began to tell me how much God loved me and His hand was upon my life. She said "Don't be afraid, just trust Him with your life and He will reveal Himself to you more and more in the future." Those words she spoke literally transformed my life. Incidentally, that young woman came out of her house to get me just in time. It was 3:00 am and my daughter and I were cold and crying. I had seriously considered going back to the Chuck's house, which I know now, would have been the cause of my death.

    The young woman allowed me and my daughter to stay in her home for a couple of days. During the time I stayed in her home, she spoke life, encouragement and hope to me. Another lady from her church came to pick us up and transported us to a Christian women's shelter. It was while I was there that I experienced the unconditional love of God. The staff was very compassionate and treated me with lots of dignity and respect. I went to early morning worship service and daily bible study and thus began my journey with the Lord.

Two weeks after I gave my heart and life to Jesus, I moved to Milwaukee, Wisconsin with my sister, Teddy Bear, and her husband Edward, the praying preacher. The more I talked to God, the more His love flooded my soul with indescribable joy. I had never experienced so much peace and acceptance in all my life. The pain that had plunged so deep within my soul was being replaced with the peace of God. The emptiness and void inside me was finally gone. Jesus Christ, the son of the Living God, had come to live within me, and to take up a permanent residence in my heart.

"God commended His love towards us, in that while we were yet sinners, Christ died for us. Much more being now justified by His blood, we shall be saved from wrath through him. For if when we were enemies, we were reconciled to God by the death of His Son, much more, being reconciled, we shall be saved by His life." (Romans 5: 8-10)

I was seventeen years old when my Lord found me and pulled me out of hopelessness and depression. All I had to give was a torn apart, broken heart; but in return, My Lord gave me joy that can never be told. In return, He gave peace that was more precious than gold. So whatever you have to give, give it in Jesus name, and He will make something beautiful out of your life. My friend,

"the thief cometh not, but for to kill, steal, and destroy. Jesus has come that we might have life and have it more abundantly." (John 10:10)

God's purpose and desire is that you will come into a covenant relationship with Him, but it is only through accepting His dear son, Jesus Christ, as your Lord and Savior. By faith, complete trust and assurance in God, you can experience a new life and be assured that heaven will be your eternal destination. The key to releasing the power of God in your life is true repentance. If you have true godly sorrow for all of your sins, Christ will transform your life.

> *"Therefore if any man be in Christ, he is a new creature: old things are passed away; behold, all things are become new. And all things are of God, who hath reconciled us to himself by Jesus Christ, and hath given to us the ministry of reconciliation." (II Cor. 5:17&18)*

You can make a commitment to Jesus Christ right now! Please pray this simple prayer:

> *"Lord Jesus, I come to you a sinner in need of a savior. I have realized that living my life apart from you has left me void and broken in many areas of my life. Jesus, I believe you died on the cross and shed your blood so I could be cleanse and forgiven of all my sins; Therefore, I confess with my mouth you are Lord, and I believe in my heart that God raised you from the dead according to your holy word in (Romans 10:9,10&13) I am now justified by your grace through the redemption that is in Christ Jesus (Romans 3:24) Thank you for being rich in mercy for your great love wherewith you love me even when I was dead in sin. Today you have given me new life in Christ and by your grace I am saved! For by grace I am saved through faith and not of myself for it is a free gift of God (Ephesians 2: 4&8)*

My friend, the angels and all the host of heaven are rejoicing because your name has just been written in the Lamb's book of life. You have an eternal home reserved for you in heaven.

Section 2 – Devotional: Three Women's Path To Freedom

CHAPTER 8
Girlfriend, What is your issue?

And there was a woman who had had a flow of blood for twelve years, and who had endured much suffering under [the hands of] many physicians and had spent all that she had, and was no better but instead grew worse. She had heard the reports concerning Jesus, and she came up behind Him in the throng and touched His Garment, For she kept saying, if I only touch His garments, I shall be restored to health. And immediately her flow of blood was dried up at the source and [suddenly] she felt in her body that she was healed of her distressing ailment. (Mark 5:25-29)

The Bible descriptively records a woman who had been plagued with an issue. Her plague was not widespread or highly infectious; it was a personal issue that caused her to suffer enormous pain in the privacy of her own home. Girlfriend's physical ailment was indicative of how she really felt mentally and emotionally. The continuous flow of blood was annoying and a nuisance that interfered with every aspect of her life. The blood flowing from her private part completely robbed her of a single day of beauty. She was not able to dress up in her beautiful soft magenta Sunday dress that depicted her femininity. Instead, she had to wear deep dark unattractive colors to hide the blood that leaked from within her. Day after day, this woman went to sleep hoping that when she woke up the next day, the nightmare would have ended. When the dawning of a new day came, she was drenched with coldness and the wet, foul smelling blood that flowed from her weakened and anemically ravished body.

She lost twelve years of her life because of this issue. The time she may have spent enjoying a husband was ripped away from her because of this issue which stood between her and the possible man of her dreams. The mental anguish was unbearable. The depression tormented her day and night. She had nobody to talk with or even give her a warm embrace. The silence was only a constant reminder of the haunting voices that echoed within her saying, "You are worthless, and less than a woman. You will never marry a man worth anything." The rejection was internalized causing her to believe she deserved the abuse inflicted upon her. Society had stigmatized her and banned her from all public events and her family was embarrassed and tired of explaining her issue. Truly, this woman had suffered many things. However, the story does not end there. She probably thought, "Maybe if I could find a plastic surgeon, all of my physical flaws would be corrected, or maybe a medical doctor would surely be the answer to my dilemma." She longed just to have a normal life. She desperately went from doctor to doctor only to be depleted of all hope. She was bankrupt and in her personal famine that lasted twelve long years. Everyday, she grew worse and by the time she heard about Jesus, she was practically dead. There was something about that name "Jesus." The name seemed to restore hope and give her a reason to live. The testimonies of Jesus; raising the dead, healing the sick and restoring the mentally ill back into their right mind fueled her faith. She did not lay and waddle in a pool of pity and cry "woe is me." She commanded herself to get up and get in the 'press'. Time was of the essence and she heard that Jesus was passing by and this might be her only opportunity to receive the healing she so longed for. Being weak as a result of the loss of blood, she kept saying within herself "I have to touch Jesus, I have to touch Jesus." She was physically exhausted and emotionally drained so the only choice she had left was to crawl to Jesus for her deliverance. The voices that told her she was making a fool of herself crawling on her hands and knees were silenced when she touched Jesus' garment. I can imagine the voices saying, "You will never be free from the depression, nobody will ever love you, you are ugly and unattractive, you're worthless, stupid, and a menace to society." She touched Jesus with a heart full of faith and He released to her healing, hope, and a purpose to live. Her issue had suddenly become a memory. Her pain was erased by the unconditional love and acceptance of Jesus Christ. This woman received so much more than she ever expected and it was all because she had one true encounter with Jesus Christ.

I can identify with this woman all too well. The two commonalities we share were not just a painful past but a glorious destiny; a future full of faith. All of the pain was eradicated and in exchange, he gave both of us purpose. The plague of living with no self-esteem was replaced with a life worth living. We both realized our value and worth when Jesus released us from the shame of a sinful past. Jesus acknowledged this woman that pressed her way through a crowd to touch His garment, just as he did for me on the street corner in South Central, Los Angeles.

My dear sister, the joy that only comes from the dawning of a new day can be yours. The weeping you have endured night after night will be turned into a praise of thanksgiving. The peace that Jesus will give you from a personal relationship with Him will never end. Out of the depths of your soul, you will have the courage to confront every issue of your past that dares to threaten your destiny.

Girlfriend, what is your issue? Jesus does not discriminate! What He did for this woman in the Gospel of Mark and what He did for me, He will do it for you. What may seem impossible for you, it is possible with God. All things are possible if you can just believe.

CHAPTER 9

The Living Water

Jesus answered and said unto her, If thou knewest the gift of God, and who it is that saith to thee, Give me a drink; thou wouldest have asked of him, and he would have given thee living water. The woman saith unto him, Sir thou hast nothing to draw with, and the well is deep: from whence then hast thou that living water? Art thou greater than our father Jacob; which gave us the well, and drank thereof himself, and His children, and His cattle? Jesus answered and said unto her, whosoever drinketh of this water shall thirst again: But whosoever drinketh of the water that I shall give him shall never thirst; but the water that I shall give him shall be in him a well of water springing up into everlasting life. (John 4:10-14)

Jesus was on a mission in the previous scripture, (John 4:10-14). His journey of love led Him to a woman that was destitute and lonely at a well. Jesus and this woman's destiny intersected and her life was forever changed. This woman was ostracized and criticized by the women and men in her community. She was well known because she had a notorious reputation and many of the women in her hometown could not stand to be in her presence. The talk around town was which man she would lay with this week.

Jesus had a need, it was necessary for Him to go through Samaria. He could have taken the short cut to go through Samaria but He chose to journey the extra miles in the hot dusty desert just to meet this woman at a well. There was an appointed time in her life when she would hear the greatest news in the entire world. The words of Jesus would be life to her dying and thirsty soul. She desperately needed a drink of the "Living Water." This woman had a need that longed to be fulfilled, but Jesus also had a need. His need was to manifest the purpose in which He had come into the world. "For God so loved this world that He gave His only begotten son that whosoever believeth in Him should not perish but have everlasting life." (John 3:16) Through the eyes of love, Jesus reached out to this woman. He knew that she was in deep pain because of all of her past and present dysfunctional relationships. He was destined to bring deliverance to this woman. 1 John 3:8 says, "For this purpose was the Son of Man manifest, that He might destroy the works of the devil." The root of her pain came from her own need of being loved and accepted; she was looking for love in all the wrong places! Jesus was not ashamed to have a conversation with this woman at the well. He did not look down on her, but He encouraged her to look up to Him for healing, hope and deliverance. What Jesus said to this woman was the million-dollar question; "Give me a drink?" She was utterly amazed and shocked that a Jew would share words with a Samaritan, and a woman at that. She quickly responded by stating that Jews have no dealings with the Samaritans. What Jesus was really asking this woman was "Give me a chance at your shattered and broken life; I will heal you in every place that hurts and restore your hope and dreams of being happy." Jesus, being the revolutionary man that He was, destroyed the wall of separation and radically changed the course of organized religion according to this woman's theology. It was an honest response to an open-ended question that caused her to seize the promise of the Living Water Jesus was offering. Her response would determine her destiny. She was faced with a pivotal moment in her life that needed an immediate answer. She did not lie to Him or try to cover her issue. She had finally come to a place where she was sick and tired of being "sick and tired." However, that place also positioned her for a miracle of inner healing. This woman sadly responded to Jesus with, "Sir thou hast nothing to draw with and the well is deep, please tell me where I can get this Living Water?

A well is defined as a source of human feelings, emotions, or a pit. What she was actually saying to Jesus is "My soul is deeply wounded and my pit of despair is beyond human help. I have nothing and nobody. No one has ever cared enough about me to take the time to discuss my issues." The only source of comfort for her was a false security that came from men who only cared about their own sexual needs. After Jesus revealed to her personal information, her faith came alive. Jesus said, "For thou hast had five husbands: and the man you are living with is not your husband."

She had heard that the Messiah was coming. She thought "Maybe this Messiah will be able to tell me all the things I need to know." This woman at the well is a classic example of countless women around the world. She represents millions of women who have become dependent upon dysfunctional relationships. The addictive behavior becomes a vicious cycle that has deadly consequences.

Jesus Christ is the bread of life: "He that cometh to me shall never hunger and He that believeth on me shall never thirst again." (John 6:35) This woman at the well believed who Jesus said He was and received what He promised to give, the Living Water:

But whosoever drinketh of the water that I shall give him shall never thirst; but the water that I shall give him shall be in him a well of water springing up into everlasting life.

The Bible says in John 4:28 & 29 (Amp.) "Then the woman left her water jar and went away to the town. And she began telling the people, come see a man who has told me everything that I ever did. Can this be [is not this] the Christ? [Must not this be the Messiah, the anointed one?]"

Her well (source of human feelings and emotions) was supernaturally transformed by one true encounter with Jesus Christ. The pit of despair and dysfunction became a memory of a painful past. She had become a powerful woman full of passion for her Lord. She had finally developed enough courage and boldness to confront her adversary, MEN. She left her means of survival (the water pot) and crutch and confronted the very thing that had her bound. Only this time she said unto the MEN, "Come see a man, which told me all things that ever I did." No longer was this woman at the well labeled by society, but she was free to become all that she was created to be. Her self-esteem skyrocketed because she discovered her true identity in the light of God's eternal plan. My sister, the Living Water is never ending and ever flowing. The river is available for you, just for the asking. There is joy, peace, life, and love in the river.

> ***Ask, and it shall be given you; seek, and ye shall find; knock, and it shall be opened unto you: for every one that asketh received; and he that seeketh findeth; and to him that knocketh, it shall be opened. (Matthew 7:7)***

CHAPTER 10

You Are Forgiven

And behold a woman of the town who was an especially wicked sinner, when she learned that He was reclining at table in the Pharisee's house, brought an alabaster flask of ointment (perfume), And standing behind Him at His feet weeping, she began to wet His feet with [her] tears; and she wiped them with the hair of her head and kissed His feet [affectionately] and anointed them with the ointment (perfume). Now when the Pharisee who had invited Him saw it, he said to himself, If this man were a prophet, He would surely know who and what sort of woman this is who is touching Him...for she is a notorious sinner (a social outcast, devoted to sin.) (Luke 7:36-50)

Let's explore this part of the Gospel account. The author allows the reader to vividly view the inside of a dinner party. There came an uninvited guest who was determined to get into the presence of Jesus. She made a decision that totally changed the course of her destiny. She had heard about all of the miraculous healings that had taken place throughout her town. Her faith had become supercharged by the words she heard. She knew that taking a leap of faith (entering into the Pharisee's house) might cost her, her very life. Nevertheless, she was destined to be delivered. Each step she took prior to her entrance into the house was like climbing a gigantic mountain. Her heart was racing because of the overwhelming fear that gripped her. But she refused to let anything stop her. This sinner woman had purposed in her heart that she was surrendering all to Jesus. Her most prized possession that was near and very dear to heart was the alabaster box of perfume. She came with a sacrificial offering, symbolically declaring she was dying to her old life and totally committing her life to Jesus. As she stood behind Jesus, she took the posture of worship. She humbly bowed her knees and wept at the feet of Jesus. She came behind him, which was a public declaration that she was inferior and she was in the presence of a superior King. Through her tears, she poured out her problems and pain that life had inflicted upon her. She was hurting, broken, and totally exhausted. It was her depravation that caused her to receive her deliverance. Her act of worship was the way in which she revealed her heart which was full of gratitude. She had a revelation who Jesus really was. While all the men's eyes were gazing upon this notorious sinner, she went to the next level of worship.

But if a woman has long hair, it is her ornament and glory? For her hair is given to her for a covering. (1 Cor. 11:15, Amp)

She boldly uncovered her hair from the burka she wore and began to gently wipe Jesus' feet with her long beautiful hair. At the feet of Jesus, the lowest part of His body, she used the hair upon her head to supernaturally reveal the transformation that was taking place. Jesus' love was reaching into her pit, and positioning her to be seated in a brand new place.

But God so rich in His mercy because of and in order to satisfy the great and wonderful and intense love with which He loved us, Even when we were dead (slain) by [our own] short comings and trespasses He made us alive together in fellowship and in union with Christ. [He gave us the very life of Christ Himself, the same new life with which He quickened Him, for] it is by grace (His favor and mercy) that you are saved (delivered from and made partakers of Christ's salvation.) He raised us up together with Him

> *and made us sit down together giving us joint seating with Him in the heavenly sphere [by virtue of our being] in Christ Jesus (the Messiah, the Anointed One) For it is by free grace (God's unmerited favor) that you are saved (delivered from judgment, made partakers of Christ's salvation) through your faith. And this [salvation] is not of yourselves [of your own doing, it cannot be through your own striving] but it is a gift of God. God has revealed His plan of redemption through Jesus Christ. (Eph 2:4-6)*

As my sister was pouring out of the depths of her soul through the expression of tears, her worship moved the heart of Jesus. He responded by pouring inside of her the very things she so longed for; love, acceptance, peace, joy and a purpose for living. Jesus protected her from the poisonous venom of that old religious spirit. This was a moment in her life that nothing else mattered; however, she was being transported mentally and emotionally from the dungeon of death to the corridors of the King's place in a moment's time. The presence of Jesus made her world right-side up, and released her from the years of turmoil and torture because of her terrible past. Yes, as you have read my testimony, I too was that notorious sinner women with a past. That's right a past! My past is forever behind me! Never to be controlled by the pain and power of my past. The pain is no longer associated with the memories of my past because I have been totally healed. The Sharon Harris story is a testimony of God's grace and mercy manifested, and you too can be totally healed my sister. **And they overcame him by the blood of the Lamb and by the word of their testimony, and they did not love their lives to the death Rev.12:11.** My testimony is your victory girlfriend! Just like this sinner woman had a testimony, I am sure I can't tell it like she could; so it is with you. God wants to use you to share your testimony because many women and men will be healed through you sharing it. Not only will others be healed but it will release you from the stigma and shame society will try to stamp on you. You must get to a point in your life that you don't care about what people will think or say about you. God wants to truly give you victory over people; therefore, you can't let nothing or nobody stop you from getting into the presence of Jesus. It is only in His presence that you can discover true purpose for living. Love and acceptance in exchange for the rejection, heartache, and heartbreak life has inflicted upon you. No, for many of us, it was not at our will; maybe you were a child. Nevertheless, you may be the consenting adolescence or adult and the choices in life you had made have caused you to suffer pain and abuse. There is good news! your life can just begin, there is hope for the hopeless. If you will commit to change today, God will transform your life and empower you with His grace to follow through and complete His good work in you until you leave this earth for your eternal destination (heaven). I believe that by confessing Jesus Christ as your Lord and Savior, receiving His love, in chapter 7 and signing and dating this book, I believe God will notarize and seal it eternally and your life will be transformed forever. Please write or email me with your testimony of how this book has impacted your life. It will be such an encouragement to me personally. Get ready to receive and enjoy living your life everyday to the fullness!

C/O Evangelist Sharon Harris
Hope Alive World Outreach Ministries
PO BOX 146
Canal Winchester OH 43110
www.hope-alive.org
evangsharris@yahoo.com

Concluding Thoughts

As you have read; my life is a pretty amazing story. However, the story doesn't end on a hopeless note. My present is more powerful than the pain of my past. It has allowed me to thrust forward into God's purpose for my life. If someone would have told me 26 years ago that I could come to know joy, peace, acceptance, and the true meaning of life, I would have laughed at him or her in scorn because of disbelief.

I would go on to meet the man of my dreams, Mr. Harry Harris, Sr., with whom I have been married for over two decades. His unconditional love and sacrificial living has helped shape me into the wife and mother that God has destined me to become. His never ending positive affirmations coupled with the word of God, has dispelled the lies of the devil that would try to creep into my thoughts, tempting me to accept defeat. For I have a revelation that those who created the pain of my past don't control the pleasure of my tomorrow. God's purpose for my life has unleashed untapped potential that I didn't know existed.

I once had but a six grade education, but today I possess my G.E.D. and my college degree in Chemical Dependency & Mental Health counseling. My educational studies are directly related to God's purpose for my life. I counsel women from all cultural backgrounds and lead them to the fountain were Living Water flows. That Living Water is Jesus Christ.

Today, I am a successful business owner. I am successful not because of the annual revenue my business receives but because we have been afforded the opportunity to reach the unreachable and employ the unemployable. It has been one more resource in the battle to win a soul for the kingdom of God.

I currently serve as co-pastor/evangelist alongside of my husband Harry Harris Sr. who serves as senior pastor of Hope Alive World Outreach Ministries in Columbus Ohio. I have developed a program (with a complete manual) that guides women through the processes of spiritual wholeness in 10 practical biblical applications through a 10 week journey called ***"Sister §2§ Sister."*** As a national and international speaker, I have been privileged to proclaim the Gospel and witness the transforming power of God released upon women from all different cultures and backgrounds.

My friend, your identification is not found in a dysfunctional past life of sin, but a glorious today that the Savior has provided for you. Just as the old Sharon has been crucified with Christ, the new Sharon has risen with power and authority to accomplish any task set before me. You can rise to a new level and enjoy that abundant life everyday!